PERSONAL PRAYERS

FOR TEACHERS

A PERSONAL PRAYER BOOK

PERSONAL PRAYERS FOR TEACHERS

Brief prayers dealing with experiences
common among teachers

Karen Cropsey

DIMENSIONS
FOR LIVING
NASHVILLE

PERSONAL PRAYERS FOR TEACHERS

Copyright © 2003 by Dimensions for Living

This book is printed on acid-free paper.

Library of Congress Cataloging-in-Publication Data

Cropsey, Karen.
  Personal prayers for teachers : brief prayers dealing with experiences
common among teachers / Karen Cropsey.
      p. cm. -- (A personal prayer book)
  ISBN 978-0-687-06337-6 (pbk. : alk. paper)
  1. Christian teachers--Prayer-books and devotions--English. I. Title.
II. Series.
  BV283.T42 C76 2003
  242'.88--dc21

                                                              2002015261

Unless otherwise noted, all Scripture quotations are from the HOLY
BIBLE, NEW INTERNATIONAL VERSION ®. Copyright © 1973, 1978,
1984 by International Bible Society. Used by Permission of Zondervan
Publishing House. All rights reserved.

Scripture quotations noted NRSV are from the *New Revised Standard
Version of the Bible,* copyright 1989, Division of Christian Education of
the National Council of the Churches of Christ in the United States of
America. Used by permission. All rights reserved.

07 08 09 10 11 12—10 9 8 7 6 5 4 3 2

MANUFACTURED IN THE UNITED STATES OF AMERICA

To Arlene and Julia,
two companion teachers who
were my "sisters" in living
these experiences

CALLED TO TEACH

I will instruct you and teach you the way you should go.

—Psalm 32:8a NRSV

Lord, I have been called by you to educate, to explain, and to enlighten. I want so much to give of myself and to impart what I know. With your help, not only can I mold lives, but also I can mend them. Lord, please give me the perseverance to stay on the path you have called me to follow, and guide me as I prepare for the opportunities and challenges of each day. Amen.

PROUD TO BE A TEACHER

Do your best to present yourself to God as one approved by him, a worker who has no need to be ashamed, rightly explaining the word of truth.
—2 Timothy 2:15 NRSV

Low pay, lack of respect, violence, and dilapidated buildings have made education a career to be disdained, Father. Let me be vigilant in remembering that your grace has given me my ability to teach, and your calling has made it happen. May I be proud of the work I do and the influence I have on those entrusted to me, knowing that, though I earn little and work under conditions many would not tolerate, my contribution to these young lives is priceless. Amen.

FOR ACCOUNTABILITY TO GOD

So then, each of us will be accountable to God.
—Romans 14:12 NRSV

Lord, if teaching is supposed to be about making a difference in the lives of others, then why isn't the difference I am making more apparent? The excitement of changing lives has been replaced with the requirement of earning high achievement test scores. Help me remember that although the things I do to prepare my students academically are important, even more valuable are the things I do that will never be reflected in test data: a smile, a kind word, and a compliment for a struggling mind or a starving heart. Keep me accountable to you, Lord. Amen.

For Needed Expertise or Understanding

Then I will give you shepherds after my own heart, who will lead you with knowledge and understanding.
—Jeremiah 3:15

For every matter has its time and way, although the troubles of mortals lie heavy upon them.
—Ecclesiastes 8:6 NRSV

Had I known, Lord, that teaching essentially requires me to be a master of all subjects and of all instructional procedures, my career path might have been different! Guide my steps through subjects and lesson plans that are unclear to me. Instill in me understanding of the concepts my students are required to master, and give me the ability to explain them appropriately and effectively. Amen.

FOR CONFIDENCE

No one will be able to stand up against you all the days of your life. As I was with Moses, so I will be with you; I will never leave you nor forsake you.

—Joshua 1:5

Influencing minds is a monumental task. Each day I realize the responsibility placed before me, the power invested in me to nurture and model, and it leaves me fearful of failure. Stand by me, Lord. May your daily presence give me confidence and the ability to teach in a caring, kind, and loving way. Amen.

FOR PEACE
ON A BUSY MORNING

Peace I leave with you; my peace I give you.
—John 14:27

My mornings are so hectic, Lord. Preparing breakfast, packing lunches, hurrying family members, checking the day's to-do list, coordinating schedules, and gathering needed teaching materials for the day at school create havoc as the day begins. As I take time for a moment of silence, remind me of your constant presence and give me your peace— peace I may carry with me throughout the busy-ness of the day, giving praise and thanks to you, my Sustainer. Amen.

For Using Time Wisely

There is a time for everything, and a season for every activity under heaven.

—Ecclesiastes 3:1

You have given me twenty-four hours, Lord, to use or abuse—the choice is mine. I will never have the opportunities of this day again. Help me remember this as I make decisions about how to spend the precious minutes of this day, realizing they are a gift from you—given so that I may celebrate your greatness and make use of the talents you have bestowed upon me. Amen.

FOR ADAPTABILITY

To accept their lot and find enjoyment in their toil—this is the gift of God. For they will scarcely brood over the days of their lives, because God keeps them occupied with the joy of their hearts.
—Ecclesiastes 5:19b-20 NRSV

Do everything without complaining.
—Philippians 2:14

*O*nce again, Lord, my planning went awry today. There is always something that must be changed. Thank you for my ability to alter schedules without warning, and for the spirit to do it willingly in the best interests of the students. Jesus himself was asked to change the water to wine at a time that was not convenient! Remind me that complaining is useless and that my energies are better spent on accepting the inevitable and proceeding to the best of my ability. Amen.

For Avoiding Favoritism

My brothers and sisters, do you with your acts of favoritism really believe in our glorious Lord Jesus Christ? —*James 2:1 NRSV*

It is so easy, Lord, to love some students more than others. An appealing smile, an unhappy home, or a unique sense of humor—all draw me to specific individuals. I am human, Lord, and cannot help myself. Control my subjectivity and replace it with objectivity. Amen.

For Accepting Each Student as an Individual

To each is given the manifestation of the Spirit for the common good. To one is given through the Spirit the utterance of wisdom, and to another the utterance of knowledge according to the same Spirit, to another faith by the same Spirit, to another gifts of healing by the one Spirit. . . . All these are activated by one and the same Spirit, who allots to each one individually just as the Spirit chooses. —1 Corinthians 12:7-9, 11 NRSV

Sometimes I forget that each student is a "someone," Lord. Each student is a person who may or may not be fed, bathed, tucked in bed at night, wanted, or loved. Help me remember this as I work with individual personalities, making allowances and understanding that students bring their whole selves to school, not just their homework. Amen.

For Laughter

Sarah said, "God has brought me laughter, and everyone who hears about this will laugh with me."
—Genesis 21:6

A giggle, a chuckle, a grin, a guffaw—laughter makes the day feel good. Thanks so much, Lord, for smiles—and for the ability to gently poke fun at our mistakes, our idiosyncrasies, and ourselves. Moments of levity transform the seriousness of lessons into a satisfying learning environment. Encourage a place for these moments during each school day. May my students always laugh with me! Amen.

FOR A PURE HEART

Above all else, guard your heart, for it is the wellspring of life. —*Proverbs 4:23*

Angry parents, surly children, demanding administrators, and uncooperative coworkers hamper my resolve to maintain a pure heart. The development of the minds entrusted to me will fall behind unless I put aside these influences. Heighten my awareness of impure influences, Lord. Allow me to ignore them so that I may teach as I should—with a pure heart. Amen.

For Gentle Authority

For in Christ all the fullness of the Deity lives in bodily form, and you have been given fullness in Christ, who is the head over every power and authority. . . . Therefore, as God's chosen people, holy and dearly loved, clothe yourselves with compassion, kindness, humility, gentleness and patience.

—Colossians 2:9-10; 3:12

A position of authority is dangerous if I forget to recognize you, Lord, as donor of my authority. Help me restrain personal pride in deference to spiritual reverence. Remind me that power in the classroom is a gift—not to be abused, but to be used gently in order to maintain an atmosphere of discipline that allows minds to flourish. Amen.

FOR HUMILITY

That is why, for Christ's sake, I delight in weaknesses, in insults, in hardships, in persecutions, in difficulties. For when I am weak, then I am strong.
—2 Corinthians 12:10

Sometimes, Lord, we think that because we teach, we are better than those who can't or don't teach. Each time a student corrects an error I have made, each time I admit that I don't know something, I learn a lesson in humility. Help me remember that only you are perfect, and that my acceptance of my imperfections enables me to be approachable—and, more important, pleasing in your sight. Amen.

For Diligence in Doing "Homework"

God is not unjust; he will not forget your work and the love you have shown him as you have helped his people and continue to help them. We want each of you to show this same diligence to the very end, in order to make your hope sure. —Hebrews 6:10-11

Lord, it seems I never leave school without papers to grade, projects to review, and manuals to read. Dragging work home is a daily task for me. Although I don't relish doing "homework," help me remain diligent in planning and preparing for class. May I not be jealous or resentful of other teachers who seem to have little or no homework of their own, remembering that outside preparation and planning will enable me to do the quality work you expect of me. Amen.

FOR DEDICATION TO CONTINUING EDUCATION

The beginning of wisdom is this: Get wisdom, and whatever else you get, get insight.

—Proverbs 4:7 NRSV

The challenge of teaching is that you are never through learning! Just once, Lord, I would like to rest my mind, but vigilance does not allow this. Help me keep abreast of new teaching techniques, current research, current events, and the latest developments in technology. Unless I require the same kind of dedication to learning from myself that I require from my students, I will stagnate. In my pursuit of knowledge, may I also gain wisdom—the wisdom that comes from you alone. Amen.

FOR SAFETY ON A FIELD TRIP

You alone, O LORD, make me dwell in safety.
—Psalm 4:8b

This is what the LORD says: "Stand at the crossroads and look; . . . ask where the good way is, and walk in it." *—Jeremiah 6:16*

Leaving the building for an opportunity to learn in another environment is always a delight, Lord. While we are out, watch over us. Help me keep my lambs within the fold, just as you do. Keep us safe, and help us remember that your arms will shelter us as we travel, and your staff will keep us together. Amen.

BEING A GOOD EXAMPLE FOR STUDENTS

Set an example for the believers in speech, in life, in love, in faith and in purity. —*1 Timothy 4:12*b

There's no question that I am a model for my students, Lord. They are extremely conscious of my actions, my manners, my words, and even my clothes. I realize that my behavior and appearance set the tone in my classroom. May my reputation in the classroom always be indicative of my demeanor, and may my example always be a positive, direct link to student progress. Amen.

BEING BOTH A PARENT AND A TEACHER

By day the LORD directs his love, at night his song is with me—a prayer to the God of my life.
                                        —Psalm 42:8

Let the word of Christ dwell in you richly as you teach and admonish one another with all wisdom, and as you sing psalms, hymns and spiritual songs with gratitude in your hearts to God. And whatever you do, whether in word or deed, do it all in the name of the Lord Jesus, giving thanks to God the Father through him.
                                        —Colossians 3:16-17

God of my life at home and at school, help me juggle my roles as teacher and parent so that I may be the best teacher and the best parent I can be. Though both my children and my students need me to love, nurture, and guide them, their specific needs are different and require different approaches. Help me remember to "change hats" each time I change settings, so that I can be all I need to be in each place. May these precious ones who depend on me, at home and at school, experience your love through me. Amen.

FACING THE DAY
WITH A GOOD ATTITUDE

In the same way, count yourselves dead to sin but alive to God in Christ Jesus. —Romans 6:11

I know it will be cold and damp at school today. There are no aides to help me today, and the weather will not allow an outside recess. Our usual schedule will be altered with programs and school pictures. Change my attitude from negative to positive as I travel to school. Help me accept the inevitable and have a good day! Amen.

KEEPING AN ORGANIZED CLASSROOM

For though I am absent from you in body, I am present with you in spirit and delight to see how orderly you are and how firm your faith in Christ is.

—Colossians 2:5

S ometimes, God, teaching is anticipating— knowing where materials are, having supplies ready, and being prepared with the tools of learning. Help me remember that you delight in order, organization, forethought, and planning so that the work of learning can proceed in a disciplined and timely manner. Amen.

TEACHING A DIFFICULT CONCEPT

We have this hope, a sure and steadfast anchor of the soul. —*Hebrews 6:19 NRSV*

You have helped me prepare for teaching by learning and living, Lord. Help me draw upon this background, as there are book lessons that I must teach today that are difficult and demanding for the students. Be my anchor as I explain and give young minds the readiness to grasp the knowledge I am required to present today. Amen.

GIVING A TEST

Not only so, but we also rejoice in our sufferings, because we know that suffering produces perseverance; perseverance, character; and character, hope.
—Romans 5:3-4

As the students take a test today, let them see that their hard work and study is a real-life lesson—that efforts put forth and hours of study result in a challenge conquered, not just knowledge gained. Show them that preparing for a test is like preparing for life. When they take time to practice, think, and study—instead of playing and relaxing—they are building a foundation of discipline necessary to complete the work of everyday living. Amen.

PREPARING
REPORT CARDS

"This is what the LORD Almighty says: 'Administer true justice; show mercy and compassion to one another.' "
—Zechariah 7:9

Evaluating a student's progress is a weighty obligation. The letters and numbers I transcribe can result in serious consequences. Help me to be a thoughtful recorder while being an accurate reporter, ever mindful of the individual. Aftereffects for report cards ripple, Lord, and may I be always mindful of this. Amen.

HANDLING
FUND-RAISING

The work is being carried on with diligence and is making rapid progress under their direction. —Ezra 5:8

[One] who gathers money little by little makes it grow.
—Proverbs 13:11b

L ord, it's that time again—time to collect money raised by the students to purchase needed supplies and materials for our school. Though it often is a frustrating task, help me remember that these funds provide my colleagues and me with the resources we need to do our jobs. Give me patience to see beyond the money envelope and the instruction time lost. Instill within me a grateful attitude for these students who have worked hard to raise this money for educational necessities. Amen.

STANDING FIRM FOR EXCELLENCE

[Jesus] replied, "You of little faith, why are you so afraid?" —Matthew 8:26a

High performance standards and scholarship demands take their toll on me, Lord. I know it's right to require my students to strive for excellence, but why must this requirement often result in a battle with parents? Neatness, accuracy, good work habits, correct spelling and grammar—all are skills needed in the business of daily living. Help parents to see that performance and scholarship standards stem from a concern for students' progress, not from a petty concern with detail. Amen.

Letting Happiness Show

A happy heart makes the face cheerful, but heartache crushes the spirit. —Proverbs 15:13

Happy are the people who know the festal shout, who walk, O LORD, in the light of your countenance; they exult in your name all day long, and extol your righteousness. —Psalm 89:15 NRSV

Lord, this day gives me an opportunity that I will never have again—and that's a sobering thought. Help me choose to smile and be happy, knowing these twenty-four hours are a sacred trust. Even if my smile or joyful attitude touches just one heart, perhaps it will help to heal a spirit—including my own. Amen.

Preparing for a Student Performance or Program

Your love has given me great joy and encouragement, because you, brother, have refreshed the heart of the saints. —*Philemon 1:7*

Dear God, preparing for a student program is a mountain of work. Yet I know that when the students perform, all the hours of preparation will be secondary to their excitement and to the delight of the audience. Instead of whining about rehearsing for an upcoming student performance, may I recognize the joys and benefits to be had both by the performers and by those witnessing this showcase of student talent. Help me encourage and uplift the students, Lord, so that it may be a successful and enjoyable experience for all. Amen.

PREPARING FOR HOLIDAYS

Look, there on the mountains, the feet of one who brings good news . . . ! Celebrate your festivals, O Judah. —*Nahum 1:15*

God, the world outside creeps into the classroom. Help me not to ignore it but to delight in the opportunities to celebrate with the students. Show me ways to correlate lessons of history and math, science and English, with the holiday at hand. May special days of the calendar become a springboard for ideas instead of a distraction. Amen.

AFTER A BAD DAY

The LORD is near to the brokenhearted, and saves the crushed in spirit. —Psalm 34:18 NRSV

*G*od, what went wrong today? The students were unsettled, and there were so many interruptions—a fire drill, announcements, knocks on the door. Lessons I thought were so well prepared were neither understood nor heeded. Heal my broken spirit, rest my mind, and give peace to my soul so that I may face tomorrow with renewed energy and a fresh spirit of excitement. May there be fewer distractions. And please bestow on my students the desire to listen, to learn, and to comprehend. Amen.

WHEN BORED WITH THE CURRICULUM

Then I was beside him, like a master worker; and I was daily his delight. —*Proverbs 8:30 NRSV*

Another day to repeat a lesson taught many times over. How can I face the same thing again? Keep me focused on you, Lord. Help me remember that though you have watched humankind struggle since the beginning of time, you never give up, even in your despair. Help me be the master worker today, delighting in a lesson that I have repeated so often yet these students have never heard. May the Rabbi be my inspiration, for he never wavered, no matter how tired, to teach the masses the lessons you sent him to share. Amen.

TEACHING DIFFICULT STUDENTS

Now for a little while you may have had to suffer grief in all kinds of trials. These have come so that your faith—of greater worth than gold, which perishes even though refined by fire—may be proved genuine and may result in praise, glory and honor when Jesus Christ is revealed.   *—1 Peter 1:6-7*

Students who delight in defying discipline create disorder. Why does it seem that these agitators are always assigned to me? Give me a new perspective in dealing with disruptive pupils. Allow my faith in Christ to tolerate the irritation of disciplining those intent on disturbing serious classmates. May my attitude toward their behavior not color my ability to teach them—and to love them—regardless of their actions. Amen.

TEACHING
GIFTED STUDENTS

We have different gifts, according to the grace given us.
—Romans 12:6

Omniscient One, your gift of knowledge and the ability to create was intended as a blessing. May those whom you have given exceptional intellectual ability and creative talents cherish their individual gifts and use their abilities with humility for your glory. Help me to encourage and instruct these students so that they may develop to their full potential as you intended. Amen.

FOR STUDENTS WHO ARE DIFFICULT TO LOVE

"See that you do not look down on one of these little ones. For I tell you that their angels in heaven always see the face of my Father in heaven."

—*Matthew 18:10*

I know, God, that you teach us to love all the children. Sometimes, though, it's hard to overlook attitudes, appearances, and circumstances that make it difficult to love a child. Remind me that you died for all—even those students who are difficult to love. Amen.

For a Student in Need

Suppose a brother or sister is without clothes and daily food.
—James 2:15

A parent offered a winter coat today to a student in need. Shivering children cannot progress—nor can children who are ashamed to come to school without clothes that are warm, clean, and appropriately sized. Thank you for the parent who gave the coat—and for reminding me that unless physical needs are met, no learning can occur. Amen.

FOR A STUDENT WHO HAS LOST A LOVED ONE

But we do not want you to be uninformed, brothers and sisters, about those who have died, so that you may not grieve as others do who have no hope.
—1 Thessalonians 4:13 NRSV

Losing a loved one is a very difficult experience for anyone, especially a young student. It's hard enough dealing with the loss—let alone missing class and trying to make up work. May I show sympathy and kindness, offering a listening heart and loving words to help my student cross the bridge of sadness. Amen.

For Student Athletes

Everyone who competes in the games goes into strict training. They do it to get a crown that will not last; but we do it to get a crown that will last forever.
—1 Corinthians 9:25

Lord, make our athletes aware that the arena is larger than the field of play, and that your way is the trophy to be prized. The contest of ability is so fleeting; the moment of triumph in the winner's circle lasts but a blink. Help our athletes to remember that the real competition is fought on the field of life, and that is where the most important game of all is played. May we all remember that a trophy awarded by you is everlasting, but an earthly crown is easily challenged. Amen.

GIVING THANKS
FOR A COWORKER

A friend loves at all times. —*Proverbs 17:17*

Sharing with a colleague, Lord, enables me to delight in my job. Thanks for sending me a kindred spirit with whom I can share teaching strategies, personal triumphs, and heartaches. Without my friend, my teaching load and my heart would be so much heavier. Amen.

Dealing with a Difficult Coworker

Beloved, do not grumble against one another, so that you may not be judged. See, the Judge is standing at the doors! —*James 5:9 NRSV*

No matter what I say or do, no matter how hard I try, it is never enough for my coworker. Even though my smiles are ignored, my kind words are met with harshness, and my compliments are followed by sarcasm, let me continue to try to break down the barrier. I know that my efforts may never result in harmony, but my actions will reflect my beliefs and, more important, glorify you. Amen.

For a Colleague Who Is Leaving or Retiring

"Let the beloved of the LORD rest secure in him, for he shields him all day long, and the one the LORD loves rests between his shoulders." —Deuteronomy 33:12

My teacher friend is leaving, Lord. I will miss her smile, her encouragement, and her companionship. By listening to my joys and heartaches and allowing me to bare my soul, she encouraged me to be the person you intend me to be and the teacher you want me to become. She instilled in me a desire for excellence. Help me continue to strive toward this goal; and help me rejoice for her, rather than to be sad at the loss of my companion. Allow me to continue honoring our friendship by maintaining the standards she helped me set for myself and my students. Amen.

FEELING LEFT OUT

We loved you so much that we were delighted to share with you not only the gospel of God but our lives as well, because you had become so dear to us.
—1 Thessalonians 2:8

If they knew how hurt I feel when I'm left out, perhaps my coworkers would not act so thoughtlessly. By sharing only with one another and never with me, ignoring me at lunch time, and never asking my desires, they create unnecessary barriers. Open their eyes, Lord, to their actions and to my hurt. Help them to see that exclusion is elitist and inclusion is professional courtesy. Amen.

WHEN HAVING
PERSONAL PROBLEMS

Now may the Lord of peace himself give you peace at all times in all ways.   *—2 Thessalonians 3:16a NRSV*

I am concerned about my friend across the hall. Things are not well in her home—or with her soul. Heavenly Father, give her the strength to climb this mountain step by step, knowing that when she reaches the peak she will be closer to you, and stronger physically and emotionally for having made the journey. May I be an "innkeeper" for her, opening my door and inviting her in, just as an innkeeper of Bethlehem gave refuge to Joseph and Mary so many years ago. Amen.

WHEN HAVING UNPLEASANT THOUGHTS ABOUT A STUDENT OR PARENT

Finally, beloved, whatever is true, . . . honorable, . . . just, . . . pure, . . . pleasing, . . . commendable, if there is any excellence and if there is anything worthy of praise, think about these things. —*Philippians 4:8 NRSV*

"But if it reappears in the clothing, or in the woven or knitted material, or in the leather article, it is spreading, and whatever has the mildew must be burned with fire. The clothing, or the woven or knitted material, or any leather article that has been washed and is rid of the mildew, must be washed again, and it will be clean."
—*Leviticus 13:57-8*

Unpleasant thoughts about students and parents are like dirty laundry; the stain remains until it is treated and washed away. Help me treat my thoughts about difficult students or parents with the soap of your love and the bleach of your forgiveness. Let my newly cleansed thoughts signal a new relationship and a new beginning with the individual or individuals who, intentionally or not, caused these stains of hurt or anger. Amen.

FOR ENCOURAGEMENT TO KEEP ON KEEPING ON

"The LORD your God is with you, he is mighty to save. He will take great delight in you, he will quiet you with his love, he will rejoice over you with singing."
—*Zephaniah 3:17*

It seems I spend all my days in this schoolroom, and carry part of it home with me every night. It seems I'm never through—never able to retreat to a place of solitude to relieve the burdens of teaching and caring for students. Lord God, place your hand of rest on my breast, still my heart, quiet my thoughts, and surround me with your peace. Amen.

GIVING THANKS FOR A KIND GESTURE

Therefore encourage one another and build up each other, as indeed you are doing.
—1 Thessalonians 5:11 NRSV

I do not cease to give thanks for you as I remember you in my prayers. *—Ephesians 1:16 NRSV*

It is not often that a parent takes a moment to offer words of thanks and appreciation. Receiving such a note today has stirred my soul and given me encouragement. This affirmation makes my soul smile; it confirms who I am and what I am attempting to accomplish in my students' lives. For this kind gesture, Lord, I offer my thanks and appreciation. Amen.

WHEN A SUBSTITUTE IS NEEDED

Let the discerning get guidance. —*Proverbs 1:5b*

Substitute teaching is a difficult task at best. Students take advantage of the substitute's ignorance of policies and procedures. Best behaviors are replaced by pranks and unruliness. Walk beside my sub, today, Lord, giving patience in dealing with rambunctious youth who carelessly misbehave and purposefully misinterpret rules, guidance for interpreting lesson plans, and laughter in the face of adversity. Amen.

WHEN A LESSON
ISN'T WELL RECEIVED

But they did not understand what [Jesus] meant and were afraid to ask him about it. —Mark 9:32

Jesus used this figure of speech, but they did not understand what he was telling them. Therefore Jesus said again . . . —John 10:6-7a

Comfort me, dear Lord, in the knowledge that even you had to speak twice—sometimes many times—before your message was understood. Today my message went unheeded. Open my eyes so that I may see a better way as I follow your example and try again, in a different way, to make my message understood. Amen.

WHEN GIVEN AN EXTRA WORK ASSIGNMENT

Diligent hands will rule, but laziness ends in slave labor   *—Proverbs 12:24*

I have so much to do, Lord, and yet another responsibility has been assigned to me! Help me to see that I was chosen for my knowledge and ability, and let me not think of this new assignment as punishment for being competent. Help me tackle this job with joy, realizing that my work will benefit many when it is completed. Amen.

WHEN ASSIGNED TO TEACH A DIFFERENT GRADE

Listen, I tell you a mystery: We will not all sleep but we will all be changed. —1 Corinthians 15:51

And whatever you do, whether in word or deed, do it all in the name of the Lord Jesus, giving thanks to God the Father through him. —Colossians 3:17

Lord, being tired of teaching a particular grade level is like being asleep. Sometimes we're not even aware that we're in that state, or even close to it. Help me to see this new grade assignment as refreshment after sleep—as a reawakening to an exciting dawn in my life and career. Whether or not this change is welcome now, quicken my heart to the exciting possibilities you have in store for me in this new assignment. Amen.

For a Principal

He tends his flock like a shepherd: He gathers the lambs in his arms and carries them close to his heart; he gently leads those that have young.   —Isaiah 40:11

Like the job of a shepherd, a principal's position is challenging, but rewarding. It includes responsibilities to administrators, staff, children, and parents. Because it is difficult to be responsive to every need and to be available at all times, help our principal to prioritize and diligently attend to the tasks at hand this day. Guide our principal in pleasing the school community and in making decisions that are in the best interests of the students. Amen.

For a Teacher in a Public School

"I revealed myself to those who did not ask for me; I was found by those who did not seek me."

—Isaiah 65:1

The Constitution says church and state must be separate, Lord, yet my Christian values still must be evident if I am to be a beacon for my students. In my dress, my words, my actions, and my professionalism, allow me to reveal my commitment to you and to show that you are the one who enables me to be who I am in the classroom. Amen.

FOR A TEACHER IN A CHRISTIAN SCHOOL

Enter his gates with thanksgiving and his courts with praise.   —*Psalm 100:4*

Lord, I enter the school doors again today with a song of thanksgiving in my heart. I am so blessed to teach in an environment where I can share your Word freely, pray openly, and practice my faith and salvation without fear of reprisal. Hallelujah, Jesus! Amen.

FOR A PRESCHOOL OR KINDERGARTEN TEACHER

Hear, my child, and accept my words, that the years of your life may be many. —*Proverbs 4:10 NRSV*

S tarting these little ones on the right path is such a joy, Lord. Their minds are untilled soil, fresh and fertile. May my labors sow wonder in learning that will grow and bear fruit all the days of their lives. Help me to keep the weeds of indifference at bay, and to hoe and harrow these young minds so that their desire to know will blossom. Amen.

FOR AN ELEMENTARY SCHOOL TEACHER

Train children in the right way, and when old, they will not stray. —Proverbs 22:6 NRSV

Dear Lord, the youngest members of your kingdom are the most impressionable and vulnerable. The charge you have given to those of us who teach them is a joyful responsibility. Help us remember our roles as models for your kingdom while these precious ones are in our care. Let us not forget that you have requested that these little ones be brought to you, and help us do just that as we present our daily lessons. Amen.

FOR A MIDDLE SCHOOL OR JUNIOR HIGH TEACHER

I have taught you the way of wisdom; I have led you in the paths of uprightness. —*Proverbs 4:11 NRSV*

Patient God, preteens are such a challenge to teach and motivate. Being too old to play and too young to drive leaves few outlets for energy. Peer acceptance often takes precedence over adult authority and educational experience. May those of us who educate these emerging young adults remember that although their butterfly wings are small, they will grow strong with patience, nurturing, and the freedom to take flight. Let us love enough, nurture enough, and trust enough not to smother flight but to smooth it with a gentle push. Soothe our minds, temper our tongues, and revive memories of our own days of puberty so that we may be participants in your plan, helping students grow, mature, and flourish. Amen.

For a High School Teacher

Hold on to instruction, do not let it go; guard it well, for it is your life. —Proverbs 4:13

God in heaven, we are the teachers who crack the cocoon and allow the butterfly to fly away to adulthood and maturity. May we have your touch as we prepare these young adults for the path you have chosen for each of them—be it college, technical school, the home, military service, or the workplace. This burden is a heavy one, for we have made the transition ourselves and have an inkling of what is in store for these young people who are so eager to enter the world. We lean on you to make the burden lighter for us. Allow us to shower our students with the confidence and knowledge to go forth into your kingdom and succeed. Amen.

FOR A UNIVERSITY TEACHER

It was he who gave some to be apostles, some to be prophets, some to be evangelists, and some to be pastors and teachers, to prepare God's people for works of service, so that the body of Christ may be built up.
—*Ephesians 4:11-12*

My Rabbi, my Teacher, the higher education setting is an important training ground for life. As a professor, I am charged with opening, encouraging, and training these promising minds that are knocking at the door to the future. Enable me to recognize that my gift of teaching in the university setting is a trust bestowed by you to prepare my students for a life in your presence, dedicated to your service. Amen.

FOR A SUNDAY SCHOOL TEACHER

So I say, live by the Spirit, and you will not gratify the desires of the sinful nature. —*Galatians 5:16*

Father in heaven, I have the joyous responsibility of teaching Sunday school. Help me explain your commandments, accurately interpret your Word, and live the life you would have me live so that I may teach not only with words, but also by example. Amen.